STRAIGHT TALKING

Inhalants

Sean Connolly

A⁺
Smart Apple Media

Published by Smart Apple Media
2140 Howard Drive West
North Mankato, MN 56003

Designed by Guy Callaby
Edited by Pip Morgan
Artwork by Karen Donnelly
Picture research by Cathy Tatge

Photograph acknowledgements
Photographs by Alamy (Vince Bevan, David Hoffman Photo
Library, Bikem Ekberzade, Enigma, Peter Glass, Jennie Hart,
Janine Wiedel Photolibrary, Medical-on-Line, Network
Photographers, PHOTOTAKE Inc.), Getty Images (Pablo
Bartholomew / Liaison, John Chiasson / Liaison,
FPG / Hulton Archive, Sean Garnsworthy, Sally and
Richard Greenhill, RAMZI HAIDAR / AFP, Christian
Hoehn, Hulton Archive, Don Johnston, Zigy Kaluzny,
Vicky Kasala, Eileen Kovchok, Rod Morata, Lida Pines,
Didier Robcis, David J. Sams, Tim Graham Picture Library,
Topical Press Agency, David Young-Wolff)

Printed in China

Library of Congress Cataloging-in-Publication Data

Connolly, Sean, 1956-
Inhalants / by Sean Connolly.
p. cm. — (Straight talking)
Includes index.
ISBN-13: 978-1-58340-648-9
1. Solvent abuse—Juvenile literature. I. Title

HV5822.S65C657 2006
613.8—dc22   2006004092

First Edition

9 8 7 6 5 4 3 2 1

Contents

Children in the poorest countries can easily find chemicals to inhale.

You may have heard people at school talking about getting drunk on alcohol or getting a buzz from a drug such as marijuana or ecstasy. Perhaps their older brothers or sisters have experimented with alcohol or with one of those drugs. But the talk at school seems to be just that—talk. Or is it?

The truth is that some of your classmates are probably getting high on drugs that are more powerful than alcohol—drugs that are so powerful they can make you feel very sick or even kill you the first time you try them. These drugs are known as inhalants.

All sorts of chemical products can be found in a garden shed, garage, or cupboard under the sink. The ones that give off strong fumes can be inhaled. These poisonous chemicals are not meant to be inhaled, and most of them have labels bearing clear warnings about the dangers of doing so. But out of ignorance, daring, or simple curiosity, many young people do inhale these fumes.

Quick highs

These chemical products are meant for all sorts of purposes—gasoline for powering a lawn mower, liquids for cleaning a computer screen, or air fresheners to make a room smell better. They contain powerful chemicals that evaporate into the air, creating fumes that can make people high. The effects are quick—a person can feel them in seconds—and can cause dizziness, sleepiness, confusion, or excitement. People who inhale the fumes feel out of control in some way, as if they were drunk. They may feel anxious and panicky, or start to have hallucinations.

Dangerous lows

Getting drunk through alcohol abuse leads to problems ranging from a hangover the morning after to more serious health risks later in life. Abusing inhalants also leads to an immediate low after the high. Regular inhaling of poisonous fumes damages both the body and the mind. Some changes can be reversed if a person stops abusing inhalants. Others can lead to lasting and irreversible damage. In some cases, the first sniff of an inhalant can be fatal.

" A so-called friend of mine introduced me to inhalants. He told me and showed me that if you huff gasoline, you will get high from it. Well, being so young and not knowing any better, I started huffing [it] every day all the way up to [the age of 14]. Ever since then, I was no longer Jeremy; it was as if I was just dead to the world. "

Jeremy (not his real name), describing four years of inhalant abuse during his childhood on www.thedoctorslounge.net—a Web site of drug stories.

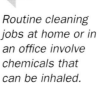

Routine cleaning jobs at home or in an office involve chemicals that can be inhaled.

You have probably seen warnings on bottles and cans of chemicals that your family uses regularly in the house or garden—products such as cleaners, lighter fluid, glue, paint thinner, and fingernail polish remover. Some labels warn that the chemicals could suddenly burst into flame or explode if they get too hot. Others warn of the dangers of getting them in your eyes or of swallowing or inhaling them.

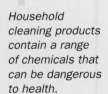

Household cleaning products contain a range of chemicals that can be dangerous to health.

Dangerous solvents

Some dangerous chemicals are a special type of liquid called solvents. They dissolve dirt and grease, so they are good for cleaning bathtubs, basins, kitchen surfaces, or sinks. Lighter fluid and gasoline are also solvents, although they are used mainly as a fuel. People risk seriously damaging their health if they inhale the fumes of these chemicals too deeply or for any length of time.

Young people sometimes experiment with inhaling these fumes in order to get high. Because most of the chemicals they inhale are solvents, this is often called volatile solvent abuse (VSA). In the 1960s and 1970s, modeling glue was often inhaled, and the problem was called glue sniffing. These glues now contain safer chemicals (see page 15).

The effects on the body

When fumes are inhaled into the lungs, chemicals are absorbed into the blood. They quickly reach the brain—usually within seconds—and can confuse the senses. People who inhale solvents often lose their balance and are unable to walk straight. They can also lose track of time or even where they are.

People who inhale solvents become unpredictable and can behave differently every time they inhale the same chemical. Sometimes they may become giggly and happy; other times they might be aggressive and violent. Unlike the effects of alcohol, which often last for hours, the feelings created by inhalants wear off quickly—usually within a few minutes. Once the effect wears off, some people may be tempted to inhale more to return to the high. To make the effects last longer, people often continue to inhale for several hours. This makes the effects stronger, but also increases the dangers.

TYPES OF INHALANTS

Inhalants can be grouped into four main categories.

Solvents
Most inhalants belong to this group of liquids, which includes paint thinners, gasoline, glues, correction fluid, and felt-tipped marker fluid.

Gases
Some inhalants are gases. Those found around the house include butane (from cigarette lighters) and propane (from gas stoves). Ether and chloroform are rarely used, as these anesthetics are available for medical purposes only.

Aerosols
Aerosols are sprays that contain solvents. Common household aerosols include spray paints, whipped cream dispensers, and hair and deodorant sprays.

Nitrites
These special chemicals, sometimes packaged in small bottles called poppers, are used in medicine, in food preservatives, and sometimes in room deodorizers. Young people rarely have access to nitrites.

The label on this household cleaner warns of the dangers and gives first-aid advice in case the cleaner is swallowed or touches the skin.

DIFFERENT METHODS OF INHALING

There are four ways of inhaling powerful chemicals. All are dangerous and possibly deadly.

There are different ways to inhale solvents or other substances. Some of the most commonly inhaled products are glues, spray paints, and cleaning fluids, which people can sniff through the nose or mouth. People either sniff the fumes from an open container or spray them directly into the nose or mouth. Huffing involves soaking a rag in an inhalant, pressing the rag to the mouth, and inhaling. A third method is bagging, or inhaling fumes from chemicals that have been poured into plastic or paper bags. This method is particularly dangerous if the bag is held over the head.

Sniffing

Bagging

Spraying

Huffing

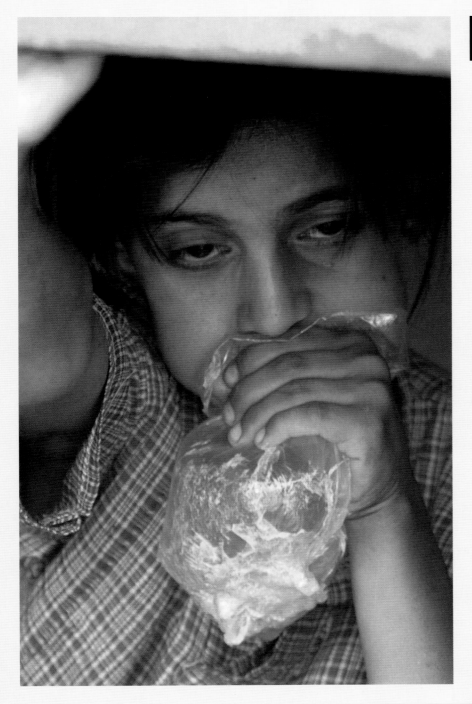

The effects of different inhalants vary, but it is possible to recognize the signs that people have been sniffing or huffing. When they have just inhaled, they often show some (or all) of the following:

● *Slurred speech*

● *Light-headedness*

● *Hallucinations or delusions*

● *Dizziness*

● *Uncontrolled laughter*

● *Agitation or anger*

● *Inability to control movements*

● *Excited behavior and then drowsiness*

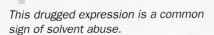

This drugged expression is a common sign of solvent abuse.

SEARCHING QUESTION

Does everyone in your family know which household products are safe and which are dangerous? Are the dangerous ones kept out of reach of small children who aren't old enough to read warning labels?

The inhalants that some young people abuse are modern products that barely existed 100 years ago. So is the problem of inhalant abuse also a modern one? Historical evidence says no—gases were inhaled in ancient Greece and by people in many countries during the 19th century.

Mysterious vapor

About 3,000 years ago, the ancient Greeks developed many ideas in mathematics, science, and politics. At the same time, they believed in many gods and spirits who could contact humans and guide their lives. For nearly 1,800 years, people traveled long distances to receive messages from the oracle at Delphi.

The oracle was a woman who sat on a stool over a deep crack in the rocky mountainside. She went into a trance before delivering a message, which was sometimes hard to understand. The writer Plutarch (A.D. 45–125) served as a priest at Delphi and believed the oracle went into a trance after inhaling vapors that came up through the rocky crack.

This idea was dismissed in 1927, when French scientists found no evidence of either a crack or a mysterious vapor. Then, in 2001, a scientific team using better equipment concluded that there had indeed

Young children's curiosity can quickly lead to danger if they are left alone, even for a few moments.

been a crack, but that earthquakes had sealed it. Further studies in the area showed that there were traces of the gas ethylene, which is known to produce hallucinations, near the site.

Laughing gas

The ancient Greeks had stumbled upon gases that affected the mind. During the Middle Ages, people produced gases using scientific advances. In 1275, Spanish chemist Raymundus Lullius discovered ether, which was later used as an anesthetic.

About 500 years later, English scientist Joseph Priestley discovered nitrous oxide, a safer anesthetic than ether (which can explode easily). Besides deadening pain, nitrous oxide changes the way people behave, often making them laugh and feel happy.

People soon realized that inhaling nitrous oxide could be fun. After taking the gas, poet Robert Southey wrote: "I am sure the air in heaven must be this wonder-working gas of delight." Demonstrators of the gas, who often asked members of their audiences to try it, toured Europe and North America. The hilarious side effects of nitrous oxide received even more publicity than the medical properties, and the anesthetic became known as laughing gas.

> " *The effect of the gas is to make those who inhale it either laugh, sing, dance, speak, or fight, and so forth, according to the leading trait of their character. They seem to retain consciousness enough not to say or do that which they would have [reason] to regret.* "

From a poster inviting members of the public to a demonstration of nitrous oxide in London on December 10, 1884.

A statue from ancient Greece shows the oracle at Delphi (seated on the right) preparing to deliver a mysterious message.

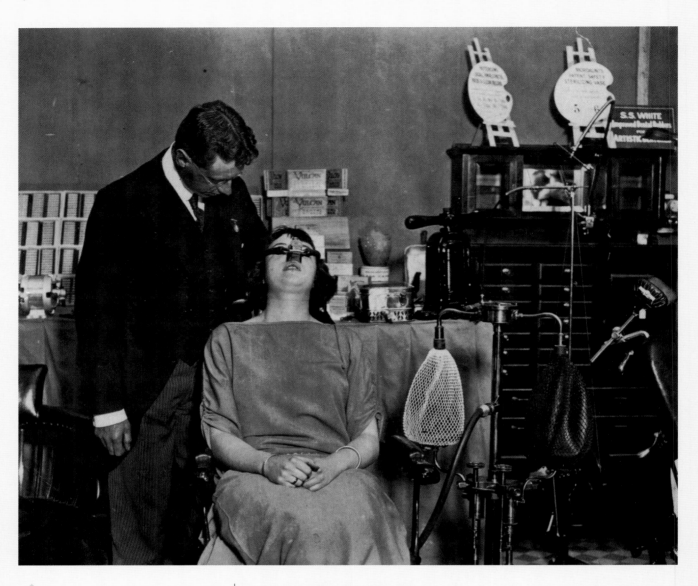

This photograph, taken about 100 years ago, shows a dentist preparing to give a patient pain-killing gas before an operation. The gas came through pipes, hoses, bags, and valves.

The problems begin

No one was too worried about a few people getting high on nitrous oxide, which was expensive and hard to obtain. Nitrous oxide became even rarer when new types of anesthetic, which could be controlled more easily and injected, were developed early in the 20th century.

In the middle of the century, the problem of inhalant abuse was first recognized. By the late 1940s, as cars became common in most countries, there were reports of young people sniffing gasoline fumes in North America, the United Kingdom (UK), Australia, and India. During the following decade, hundreds of new products were produced from oil to help with cleaning and other household tasks. These products gave young people more opportunities to experiment with inhalants.

A boy builds a model plane in the 1950s. At that time, modeling glue contained dangerous solvents.

Glue sniffing

The most popular inhalant was a chemical that seemed innocent enough and that most young people had in their own bedrooms: modeling glue. Parents and others soon learned about the dangers of glue sniffing—as any type of inhalant abuse became known—from reports on television and in the newspapers.

By the late 1960s, glue manufacturers had changed the chemical formulas for their products, either replacing toluene (the ingredient that gave off fumes) or adding other chemicals to make it harder to sniff.

One temptation had been removed, but sniffers turned from their bedroom shelves to kitchen cupboards, where dozens of other products were available. Inhalant abuse just would not go away.

" *In the 1980s, everyone knew about the problem of glue sniffing, but over the last 20 years, it has slowly slipped from public view and has been forgotten. Yet VSA continues to cause death and harm to many. With children playing Russian roulette with their lives, it is no longer tenable to ignore VSA.* **"**

Simon Blake, author of *Dangerous Highs*, a report on inhalant abuse published by the National Children's Bureau and ChildLine, June 2005.

Dancing with death

Inhalants are more than dangerous—they can be deadly. They include several types of chemicals and hundreds of household products (see pages 8–11), but none are meant to be inhaled. Inhaling just one of them can damage the throat and lungs even before it reaches the brain.

There are other risks, too. For example, someone who has just sniffed lighter fluid could light a match or toss the lighter into an open fire where it would almost certainly explode. Another person might choke or suffocate after losing consciousness. A sniffer might start a car and drive dangerously. But the most frightening risk of all is sudden sniffing death (see page 18).

Being high on inhalants makes people clumsy and less able to react quickly. Their judgment is poor, and they become accident-prone. Many young people who drown or die after a fall were abusing inhalants.

Firefighters wear special masks to protect them from fumes given off by burning chemicals.

STRAIGHT TO THE BRAIN

**The fastest way to absorb any drug is to inhale it.
This is why people smoke marijuana or sniff cocaine.
Inhalants take just a few seconds to go from the lungs
to the brain and central nervous system.**

Inhalants change the way the brain works. Sniffers or huffers become confused and dizzy at once, and their speech becomes slurred. This is often followed by a period of great excitement and recklessness, which lasts up to half an hour (depending on how much has been inhaled). Drowsiness and a lack of energy soon follow. Using inhalants leads to a hangover that lasts up to 24 hours and is often accompanied by a bad headache and a feeling of nausea.

Apart from the irritation of breathing in strong chemicals, inhalant abuse triggers many changes in the body (see pages 20–23). Some can be reversed if the person stops using inhalants; others, however, become permanent and can lead to serious illness or death.

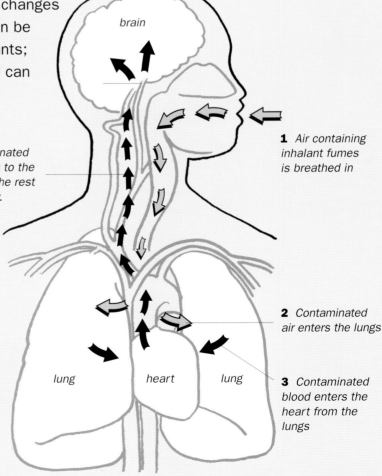

4 *Contaminated blood flows to the brain and the rest of the body.*

1 *Air containing inhalant fumes is breathed in*

2 *Contaminated air enters the lungs*

3 *Contaminated blood enters the heart from the lungs*

brain

lung   heart   lung

FACT

People who abuse inhalants have a strong smell around the mouth and nose. Just as a drinker's breath can smell of whiskey or beer, a sniffer or huffer has a tell-tale smell of gasoline, paint thinner, or other chemicals. The smell of the inhalant also sticks to their clothes for hours.

SUDDEN SNIFFING DEATH

In the United States, 100 or more young people a year die from sudden sniffing death, which is a form of heart attack. It occurs when the heart does not receive enough oxygen to work properly. This lack of oxygen can be caused by putting a plastic bag over the head while sniffing, or by inhaling a chemical that causes the throat to swell and become blocked. The heart muscle, which uses oxygen as fuel, is forced to work harder. The heart can lose its regular beat, and if the sniffer becomes excited or active (putting even more strain on the heart), it can stop beating altogether. The person dies unless emergency medical help arrives almost immediately. This type of tragic death can occur the first time someone abuses an inhalant.

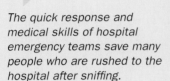

The quick response and medical skills of hospital emergency teams save many people who are rushed to the hospital after sniffing.

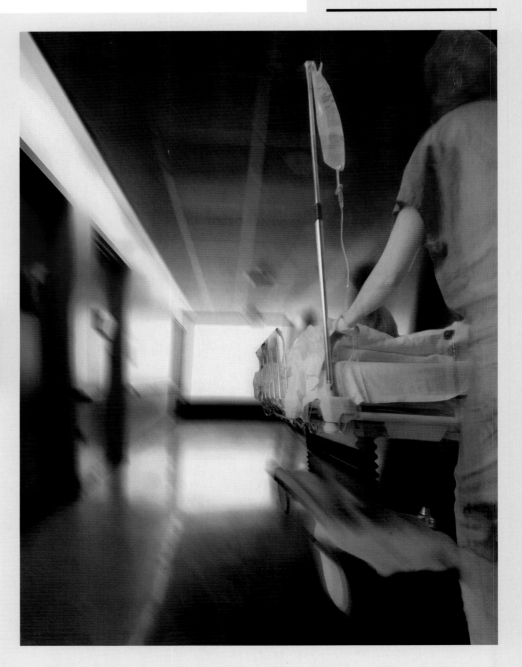

DEATHS FROM INHALANT ABUSE IN BRITAIN, 1995–2003

Year	Number of deaths
1995	77
1996	78
1997	78
1998	80
1999	75
2000	66
2001	63
2002	65
2003	51

Source: Community Health Services, St. George's, University of London.

A homeless Romanian teenager reaches out as the effects of sniffing glue start to make her feel drowsy and lethargic.

A DOCTOR'S SORROW

Richard Heiss, a family doctor in California, knew that many young people sniffed inhalants, but he and other doctors were more familiar with problems linked with heroin, cocaine, and other drugs. In 1995, Dr. Heiss learned that his 12-year-old son Wade had been found by his older brother sniffing from a can of air freshener. He lectured his son about how the gases in these products could harm the kidney and liver, and Wade promised not to do it again.

Two weeks later, Dr. Heiss was summoned home to find Wade collapsed beside the house after inhaling more poisonous fumes. The Heiss family watched with horror as the doctor tried—and failed—to revive his son. Wade died later that day, six days before his 13th birthday. Since then, Dr. Heiss has traveled widely, telling young people and health professionals about the dangers of inhalant abuse.

SEARCHING QUESTION

Do you think there is enough information available to let young people know that inhalant abuse is dangerous and can lead to death easily and quickly?

Peer pressure— not wanting to feel left out of a group—leads some young people to abuse inhalants.

Inhalant abuse can lead to all sorts of problems. Some are temporary and can be solved when someone stops sniffing, but many cause lasting damage to a person's health. Because so many different products can be abused, and because people's reactions vary, it is impossible to say that abusing an inhalant always leads to a particular problem. What is clear, however, is that every product is dangerous.

Personality changes

One big effect of abusing inhalants is a change in personality. Some changes are similar to those that are caused by drugs such as ecstasy or marijuana. For example, an inhalant abuser might drop old friends and turn to new ones who use the same drug. Other changes are linked to the particular way that getting high (and coming down) from inhalants affects the way a person thinks.

There seems to be a link between abusing inhalants and suicide. Doctors and drug experts point to the following reasons for taking this risk seriously.

● *Suicide is more common when people are high on inhalants than when they are not.*

● *Boys abuse inhalants more than girls and are among the highest-risk groups for suicide.*

● *Coming down from an inhalant high often leads to a low so deep that it becomes depression. This depression may trigger a desire to end one's life.*

● *Regular users often have emotional or psychological problems before abusing inhalants. These might become more serious.*

A boy drifts off to sleep in the library. Regular sniffing upsets the body's natural rhythms and disturbs the patterns of sleep and wakefulness.

A change in routine is one of the first signs that people are regular sniffers. They no longer eat or sleep at their usual times. They stop taking part in their favorite activities—they are too tired or else they are sniffing or huffing. They find it hard to concentrate on lessons that once seemed easy or interesting. Some abusers develop a negative attitude toward their family and friends.

Harming the body

The human body isn't designed to inhale harmful substances and can be damaged by the first sniff. People who sniff occasionally develop blisters and rashes around the mouth and nose. Their throats become raw and sore, leading to coughing and runny noses, as if they had a cold.

Once inhaled, the chemicals damage tissues throughout the body, including the brain. If people begin sniffing regularly, they show signs of hearing and memory loss and confusion, and suffer frequent headaches. Their muscles waste away, and sniffers often lose weight. The body, however, continues to try to flush out the harmful chemicals. It can do this if the person does not inhale too much or too often. Otherwise, many chemicals collect in the kidneys and liver, building up faster than they can be flushed away. That is when the real trouble begins.

Frequent headaches, coughing, runny noses.

Blisters and rashes around the mouth and nose.

Memory loss, confusion, weight loss.

NO TURNING BACK

Doctors have found clear links between the regular abuse of certain chemicals and the irreversible effects they have on the body.

● Hearing loss—toluene (in spray paints and glues) and trichloroethylene (in cleaning fluids and correction fluids).

● Uncontrolled twitching of arms and legs—hexane (in glues and gasoline) and nitrous oxide (in gas cylinders).

● Central nervous system or brain damage—toluene (in spray paints and glues).

● Bone marrow damage—benzene (in gasoline).

● Liver and kidney damage—substances containing toluene and chlorinated hydrocarbons (in correction fluids and dry-cleaning fluids).

● Loss of oxygen in the blood—organic nitrites (in poppers and room fresheners) and methylene chloride (in varnish removers and paint thinners).

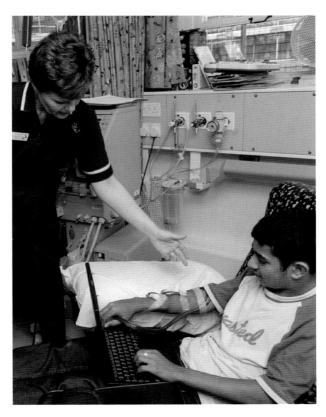

A boy with a kidney disease works while hooked up to a dialysis machine, which can take over if the kidneys are not healthy. Inhalant abusers may damage their kidneys so badly that they need dialysis, too.

SEARCHING QUESTION
Some everyday activities, such as crossing the street or swimming, can become dangerous if a person has been sniffing. Can you think of any other activities that could be risky if someone was using inhalants?

People of either sex or from any background—like these high school students—can become inhalant abusers.

There is no typical inhalant abuser. The problem affects people from all backgrounds, rich and poor, regardless of race or religion. There is no age limit. Anyone, including toddlers and young children, can find an unlocked cupboard and open a bottle or press an aerosol button.

According to the inhalant-abuse charity Re-Solve, the youngest person to die of inhalant abuse was 7 years old, and the oldest was 86. Inhalant abuse is also one of the only drug problems that affects girls as much as boys. No one can say that it could never happen in their family or area.

Why young people?

Although anyone can be an inhalant abuser, most sniffers and huffers are between 11 and 16. There are three main reasons for this link to late childhood and the early teen years.

First, people of this age cannot easily get other drugs, whether legal or illegal. Widely enforced laws in most countries make alcohol and tobacco (which many young people are tempted to try) unavailable to those under 18 or 21. People who sell illegal drugs such as marijuana, cocaine, and ecstasy (all popular with teens) know they risk particularly harsh punishments if convicted of selling to children.

Second, inhalants are available nearly everywhere, and children need not look far to find them.

A third reason is ignorance. Inhalant abuse tends to decrease by the time people reach the age of 15 or 16. By then, they have probably learned about some of the dangers involved. Also, those who sniff or huff have often acquired a bad reputation by this age. That and the widespread belief that inhalants are a dirty drug can help to convince others to end their abuse. Younger children, though, are less aware of the dangers and the poor image of inhalant abuse, especially if they begin sniffing on their own out of curiosity.

Some young people, like this boy bagging on a city street, abuse inhalants to escape poverty or boredom.

" **Me and this other girl were sniffing Liquid Paper; I didn't know what she was going to do, but she did a robbery with violence. She smashed [another female] on the head and held a knife to her throat.** "

Seventeen-year-old girl, 1992.

Thousands of children live poorly in the Brazilian city of Rio de Janeiro after escaping from the poverty or violence of their family homes. These street children rely on begging and often abuse inhalants.

Around the world

Many countries have a problem with inhalant abuse. In Sweden and Greece, for example, more teenagers experiment with inhalants than with marijuana. The opposite is true in the U.S., UK, Canada, and Australia, although many people still abuse inhalants in these countries.

Young people from poor backgrounds in nearly every country seem to be at the highest risk of abusing inhalants. Inhalant abuse is especially common in social groups that are separate in some way from the wider public. In the U.S. and Canada, for example, Native Americans and Inuits report that their young people are tempted to sniff inhalants out of boredom or because they feel they have fewer opportunities than other young people in their country. Aboriginal communities in Australia have similar stories to tell.

Some of the saddest examples of inhalant abuse come from Africa, South America, and Asia, where many people as young as eight years old live on their own, trying to find food and shelter in big cities. These street children often turn to inhalants to block out the pain and hardship in their lives.

" Rich people escape from reality using cocaine. Poor people use what they can buy: alcohol, solvents, cigars, etc. It is not only an economic problem: it is a human problem. "

Entry on www.ayn.ca message board from Iván Cuevas, Mexico City.

WHY USE INHALANTS?

The problem of inhalant abuse is mainly centered on young people, especially those who don't know about the deadly risks involved. Generally, these young people try out inhalants for one or more of the following reasons:

- *To seem tough.*

- *To try something new.*

- *Because inhalants are cheaper and easier to get than alcohol.*

- *To escape from pressure or stress.*

- *Because of peer pressure from friends.*

- *Because inhalants seem exciting.*

- *To rebel against parents or teachers.*

 Sniffing is kinda dumb. Basically you're just drowning yourself. It can give you monster headaches and make you smell really bad.

Entry from an Internet inhalants message board.

A young man sniffs solvents from a plastic bag on a bench outside a night shelter for homeless people in London.

People may experiment with inhalants out of curiosity or a wish to rebel, but surely sniffers stop once they understand the dangers—don't they? But what if they felt some sort of force pushing them to continue? They might know about the risks involved but somehow be unable to stop.

Dependence

Unfortunately, many people do find it hard—or almost impossible—to stop using inhalants. They are taking drugs and may become addicted to them. Instead of calling it addiction, doctors and drug experts prefer to use the words "dependent" and "dependence" to talk about these powerful urges. There are two kinds of dependence: physical dependence and psychological dependence. One or both kinds of dependence can develop after a person has taken a particular type of drug regularly.

This boy might think that bagging regularly is no big deal, but drug experts would be concerned about his developing habit.